BURGERS

BURGERS

David Morgan

hamlyn

Notes

A few recipes include nuts or nut derivatives. It is advisable for those with known allergic reactions to nuts and nut derivatives and those who may be potentially vulnerable to these allergies, such as pregnant and nursing mothers, invalids, the elderly, babies and children, to avoid dishes made with nuts and nut oils. It is also prudent to check the labels of prepared ingredients for the possible inclusion of nut derivatives.

The Department of Health advises that eggs should not be consumed raw. This book contains some dishes made with raw or lightly cooked eggs. It is prudent for more vulnerable people such as pregnant and nursing mothers, invalids, the elderly, babies, and young children to avoid uncooked or lightly cooked dishes made with eggs.

Both metric and imperial measurements have been given. Use one set of measurements only, and not a mixture of both.

Standard level spoon measurements are used in all recipes: 1 tablespoon = one 15 ml spoon
1 teaspoon = one 5 ml spoon

Full-fat milk should be used unless otherwise stated. Fresh herbs should be used unless otherwise stated. Large eggs should be used unless otherwise stated.

Ovens should be preheated to the specified temperature – if using a fan-assisted oven, follow the manufacturer's instructions for adjusting the time and the temperature.

First published in Great Britain in 2006 by Hamlyn, a division of Octopus Publishing Group Ltd, 2–4 Heron Quays, London E14 4JP

Copyright © Octopus Publishing Group Ltd 2006

ISBN-13: 978-0-600-61423-4

ISBN-10: 0-600-61423-9

A CIP catalogue record for this book is available from the British Library

Printed and bound in China

10 9 8 7 6 5 4 3 2 1

contents

introduction

what exactly is a burger?

The dictionary defines a burger as a sandwich consisting of a cooked beef patty in a bun that's often accompanied by a variety of other ingredients. While this description is still relevant, today the word 'burger' covers any number of permutations on this classic staple. While the burger is the ultimate choice for a quick, easy and filling bite on the go, it also graces the menus of some of the world's finest eateries, where chefs take great pride in serving up the best ingredients prepared to their own individual recipes. The burger really is wonderfully versatile and it's fair to say that it's America's – and probably the world's – favourite fast food.

the versatile sandwich

Although beef is traditionally the staple ingredient in a burger, it is by no means the only possibility and, as this book demonstrates, there are endless variations when it comes to making your own burgers, both with regards to the filling and the bread used to surround it. From minced lamb to fish and vegetables, there really are no limits, and then of course there's the decision to be made about which sauce or relish you use and what accompaniments you choose to serve with your burger. Whether you're eating it from a serviette, standing up with a paper plate or serving up something a bit special for guests, you'll enjoy searching for your perfect combination and trying out the many classic and unusual burger ideas over the following pages. So, if you thought a burger was just beef in a bun, then it's time to think again!

the history of the burger

Although we may think of the burger as being a relatively modern invention, it has, in fact, been enjoyed in various forms for many hundreds of years. It is believed that the great Mogul armies led by Genghis Khan ate meat patties while travelling on their conquering missions. With time being of the essence, they favoured food that could be eaten without the need to stop and make camp, and so ground meat patties fitted the bill perfectly. Much like today, these early burgers were favoured for convenience and the fact that they could easily be eaten with one hand while the armies continued to ride. However, they were consumed raw so they probably didn't have quite the same enjoyment factor that we expect from convenience food today.

the hamburg steak

The humble burger became gradually more appetizing over the ensuing years although, for a long time, it was still regarded as a convenient way of having a quick and filling meal using the most basic of ingredients. Despite being an American institution it's believed that the burger was originally introduced to the country via the European immigrant ships in the early nineteenth century. Germans travelling to north America from Hamburg ate Hamburg steak on the voyage. It was a popular local food that suited the conditions perfectly because it travelled well and kept for a long time as the meat was generally salted. Hamburg steak was an economical meal, as cheaper cuts of meat were made more appetizing by blending in various spices and flavourings. To make the meat go even further on board ship, other ingredients such as breadcrumbs were added and the meat patties were seared and served with bread, like a sandwich. On their arrival in America, the new immigrants kept their culinary traditions alive and the popularity of these Hamburg steaks began to spread. The name evolved into the hamburger and a great American tradition was born.

a lasting influence

The hamburger became popular at fairs and markets with stalls being set up all over the country and it wasn't long before franchises and official retail outlets were opened that sold only the popular food. Today, a town without a burger bar is a rare sight indeed, and the burger is still top of most people's quick-fix food list. As the burger gained in popularity so new variations began to crop up and people became a little more adventurous.

creating a classic

Ground beef can take other flavours well and it is easily combined with herbs, spices and flavourings before being shaped and cooked. Of course, the most popular addition to the burger was cheese and this is still the most widely consumed variation of the classic burger today. Relishes and accompaniments were also easy to add as the burger was eaten in a bun, generally with the hands, and anything that could be packed comfortably into the bun was considered appropriate. So, salad, mayonnaise, tomato relish, mustard, gherkins and onions all became regular companions to the beef burger. At the same time, individuals set about creating their own burger mixtures by seasoning and flavouring the meat in different ways to create ever more interesting takes on the basic burger.

Today, this national favourite is just as likely to be found at a stall by the side of the road as on the menu of a top restaurant and both will provide an equally enjoyable experience. In fact, in recent years, the burger has experienced a surge of popularity in restaurants, with a greater appreciation of its place in the American culinary heritage. Chefs have begun to realize the potential of this much-loved meal with its humble origins. The burger is often used as a quality benchmark for restaurants – get this right and you can rely on a loyal customer following.

making your own burgers

You may well enjoy treating yourself to a burger and fries for lunch every now and again but it's fair to say that nothing can really compare to the taste of a freshly cooked, home-made burger with all the trimmings. You have total control over the ingredients used, the quality and cut of the meat and the cooking technique and time. And let's not forget that making burgers is fun – from mixing the ingredients to shaping the patties and feeling your mouth begin to water as the smells waft from the grill, there's something immensely satisfying about tucking into your own home-made burgers.

hands on food

Kids love to get involved as making burgers can be a gloriously messy experience that requires getting your hands covered in food; they're also a great way to introduce children to new ingredients. Perhaps the most exciting thing about making your own burgers though is that the variations really are endless. There's no need to miss out if you're a vegetarian or you don't eat red meat. As this book demonstrates, there's a burger recipe to suit every taste. How about trying a Sweet Potato, Butter Bean and Feta Burger with Sun-blushed Tomato Pesto (see page 75)? Or get creative with a Crispy Tofu Burger (see page 76). If you are a meat lover then there's no need to limit yourself to beef. You'll find ideas for pork, lamb and chicken burgers as well as some great ideas for fish such as the Swordfish Steak Burger with Crunchy Orange Salsa (see page 60).

quick and convenient

As well as being extremely versatile, home-made burgers can provide healthy and nutritious meals that score high on the convenience factor, too. Many of the recipes in this book can be prepared in advance and cooked to order. In fact, a lot of the beef and other meat-based burgers will benefit from standing in the refrigerator to chill before cooking as this allows the patties to set and makes them easier to handle. As most of the recipes are quick to cook, you'll spend less time in the kitchen later on.

cooking techniques

Burgers have long been associated with barbecues and they're ideal for throwing on the grill. Condiments, relishes and accompaniments can all be set out for people to help themselves and the smoky flavour really does enhance the taste of the burger. This is true of fish and many vegetarian burgers, as well as meat. The combination of ground meat with other ingredients such as breadcrumbs or egg to bind the mixture together means that the burger is firm enough to withstand the high temperatures and rough treatment that barbecuing entails. Obviously, not all recipes are suited to this cooking technique and some of the more delicate burgers require gentler handling. These can be cooked just as easily with a little oil in a griddle or frying pan for equally delicious results.

meat

classic american

1 kg (2 lb) good quality coarsely
  minced beef

2 garlic cloves, crushed

1 tablespoon vegetable oil

8 streaky bacon rashers

a little light olive oil, for brushing

salt and pepper

To serve:

4 large burger buns

75 g (3 oz) mixed salad leaves

1 beef tomato, sliced

4 thick slices strong Cheddar cheese or
  Monterery Jack

1 small red onion, sliced into rings

1 quantity of Quick BBQ Sauce
  (see page 92)

Serves 4

Preparation time: 15 minutes, plus chilling

Cooking time: 15 minutes

This one is for adults only; with a full half pound of burger per person it's a hearty meal for any meat lover.

Mix the beef and garlic together and season well with salt and pepper. Divide the mixture into 4 equal portions and form each one into a round patty, pressing together firmly. Cover and chill for at least 30 minutes.

Grill the bacon until slightly crisp and keep it warm. Heat a griddle pan or barbecue to medium-high. Brush the burgers with a little oil and cook them for 5–6 minutes on each side, depending on how you like them cooked.

Assemble each burger by covering the base of each bun first with salad leaves then tomato slices. Place the cooked burger on the salad then top with the cheese, bacon and sliced red onion. Serve open or topped with the bun lid and accompanied with lots of quick BBQ sauce.

chorizo burger with red wine jus

500 g (1 lb) good quality coarsely
   minced beef
250 g (8 oz) spicy chorizo sausage, skinned
   and finely chopped
125 g (4 oz) chargrilled red peppers,
   finely chopped
2 tablespoons chopped flat leaf parsley
1 teaspoon smoked paprika
2 tablespoons light olive oil
½ red onion, finely chopped
1 garlic clove, crushed
1 teaspoon sugar
125 ml (4 fl oz) red wine
salt and pepper

To serve:
4 Crusty Sesame Seed Rolls (see page 84)
75 g (3 oz) rocket

Serves 4
Preparation time: 20 minutes, plus chilling
Cooking time: 15 minutes

You can buy chargrilled peppers preserved in jars from large supermarkets to save time. If you want to make your own, simply char the skin of a pepper under a grill until it's black, then wash off the blackened skin.

Mix the beef with the chorizo, red pepper, parsley and paprika. Season well with salt and pepper and divide the mixture into 4 round burgers. Cover and chill for 30 minutes.

Heat the oil in a frying pan and fry the burgers for 3 minutes on each side until slightly charred. Remove from the pan. Add the onions and garlic to the same pan and cook until softened, about 2 minutes. Next, add the sugar and red wine and simmer until the liquid has reduced by half.

Put the burgers back in the pan and cook for a further 3 minutes, turning occasionally, until the sauce is slightly sticky and the burgers are cooked through.

To assemble, toast the rolls under a grill and fill with rocket and the burgers. Spoon over the extra pan juices and serve.

sicilian burger

1 red onion, finely chopped

3 garlic cloves

625 g (1¼ lb) good quality coarsely
   minced beef

2 tablespoons chopped basil

2 tablespoons chopped marjoram

2 tablespoons chopped oregano

50 g (2 oz) freshly grated Parmesan cheese

75 g (3 oz) sun-dried tomatoes,
   finely chopped

75 g (3 oz) black olives, finely chopped

a little light olive oil, for brushing

salt and pepper

To serve:

2 Soft Focaccia Rolls, quartered
   (*see page 85*)

Basil Mayonnaise *(see page 93)*

75 g (3 oz) rocket

1 ball of mozzarella cheese, about
   125 g (4 oz)

a small bunch of basil

Serves 4

Preparation time: 20 minutes, plus chilling

Cooking time: 15 minutes

Heat the oil in a frying pan and fry the onion and garlic over a medium heat for 4 minutes or until softened. Set aside to cool. Place the beef, onion and garlic mixture, herbs, Parmesan, tomatoes and olives in a large bowl. Season with salt and pepper and mix well. Divide the mixture into 8 portions and shape each one into a ball then flatten slightly into a burger. Cover and chill for 30 minutes.

Heat a griddle pan or barbecue to hot. Brush the burgers with a little oil and cook them for 4–5 minutes on each side until slightly charred on the outside and medium in the centre.

Split the focaccia rolls in half and toast slightly on the griddle pan or barbecue. Spread the base with basil mayonnaise and top with rocket and the cooked burger. Tear the mozzarella ball into pieces and divide among the 8 burgers. Top with the lids and a basil leaf and secure with a cocktail stick. Serve with extra basil mayonnaise and rocket.

mexico city burger with avocado salsa

1 tablespoon light olive oil, plus extra
for brushing

1 onion, finely chopped

2½ tablespoons taco seasoning

625 g (1¼ lb) good quality coarsely
minced beef

2 tablespoons chopped coriander

25 g (1 oz) jalapeño peppers

1 teaspoon Tabasco sauce

salt and pepper

Avocado salsa:

1 avocado, peeled and diced

2 large tomatoes, skinned, deseeded
and diced

1 red chilli, deseeded and finely chopped

4 spring onions, thinly shredded

2 tablespoons chopped coriander

juice and grated rind of 1 lime

3 tablespoons olive oil

To serve:

4 soft tortillas

iceberg lettuce, shredded

50 ml (2 fl oz) soured cream

Serves 4
Preparation time: 20 minutes, plus chilling
Cooking time: 20 minutes

Heat the oil in a frying pan and cook the onion with the taco seasoning until soft, about 3–4 minutes. Leave to cool then season with salt and pepper and mix with the beef, coriander, jalapeño peppers and Tabasco sauce. Divide the mixture into 8 portions, shape each one into a ball then flatten out slightly. Cover and chill for at least 30 minutes.

Meanwhile, combine all the ingredients for the salsa in a small bowl. Chill to allow the flavours to develop.

Heat a griddle pan or barbecue to hot. Brush the burgers with a little oil and cook them for up to 5 minutes on each side, depending on how well you like them done.

Warm the soft tortillas under a grill. Place some of the lettuce over each tortilla then add two of the mini burgers. Top with a few spoonfuls of salsa and a dollop of soured cream. Fold the tortillas in half and serve.

pesto burger

625 g (1¼ lb) good quality coarsely
   minced beef

1 small red onion, finely chopped

2 garlic cloves, crushed

2 teaspoons dried basil

4 baby mozzarella balls or cherry
   bocconcini

4 thin slices prosciutto

a little light olive oil, for brushing

salt and pepper

Pesto:

25 g (1 oz) basil, chopped

25 g (1 oz) Parmesan cheese, grated

1 garlic clove, crushed

25 g (1 oz) pine nuts, roasted

75 ml (3 fl oz) olive oil

salt and pepper

To serve:

8 slices sourdough bread

2 tomatoes, sliced

50 g (2 oz) rocket

Serves 4
Preparation time: 30 minutes, plus chilling
Cooking time: 10 minutes

Home-made pesto is always better than bought pesto, especially the stuff in jars. If you need to buy it, get it fresh, preferably from an Italian delicatessen. If you make your own, you can either roast your own pine nuts in a pan or buy them ready-roasted.

First, make the pesto sauce. Place all the ingredients for the pesto into a food processor. Blitz until the mixture resembles a smooth sauce. Season to taste with salt and pepper, adding a little more oil if necessary.

Next, make the burgers. Mix together the beef, onion, garlic and basil in a bowl and season well with salt and pepper. Divide the mixture into 4 equal portions. Form them into balls around a piece of mozzarella then wrap each burger in a slice of prosciutto. Cover and chill for 1 hour.

Heat a griddle pan or barbecue to medium-high. Brush the burgers with a little oil and cook for about 5 minutes on each side, depending on how well you like them done.

Spread the slices of bread with a little pesto sauce and toast under a grill until golden. Top each slice with a few slices of tomato, some rocket and a burger. Drizzle each with a little pesto sauce and serve with the remaining bread slices.

blue-cheese burger

1 tablespoon vegetable oil

1 onion, finely chopped

2 garlic cloves, crushed

625 g (1¼ lb) good quality coarsely
   minced beef

2 tablespoons finely chopped chives

1 pear, peeled, cored and grated

1 tablespoon wholegrain mustard

25 g (1 oz) butter

3 field mushrooms, thickly sliced

150 g (5 oz) blue cheese

a little light olive oil, for brushing

salt and pepper

To serve:

4 thick slices walnut bread

1 bunch watercress

a few chopped chives

Serves 4
Preparation time: 20 minutes, plus chilling
Cooking time: 20 minutes

Heat the oil in a frying pan and cook the onion and garlic over a medium heat for about 5 minutes or until softened. Set aside to cool. Mix together the ground beef, the onion and garlic mixture, chives, pear and mustard. Season well with salt and pepper. Divide the mix into 4 equal portions. Form into balls then flatten slightly. Cover and chill for at least 30 minutes.

Melt the butter in a small pan and add the mushrooms. Fry for about 5 minutes then set aside to cool. Heat a griddle pan to hot. Brush the burgers with a little oil and cook them for about 5 minutes on each side, depending on how well you like them done. Divide the blue cheese into 4 portions, place them on the top of each burger then melt slightly under a hot grill.

To assemble, toast the slices of walnut bread on a hot griddle pan until lightly browned. Top each slice with the fried mushrooms and a burger. Garnish with the watercress and chives and serve immediately.

garlic butter beef burger with garlic mayo

75 g (3 oz) butter

3 garlic cloves, crushed

2 tablespoons chopped parsley

650 g (1 lb 5 oz) good quality coarsely
   minced beef

100 g (3½ oz) sun-dried tomato, finely
   chopped

1 tablespoon Dijon mustard

1 tablespoon light olive oil, for cooking

salt and pepper

To serve:

4 large burger buns

rocket

1 quantity Garlic Mayonnaise *(see page 93)*

Serves 4

Preparation time: 25 minutes, plus chilling

Cooking time: 10 minutes

Mix the butter with the garlic and parsley. When well combined, spoon on to a piece of greaseproof paper and roll up into a thick cylinder shape. Chill for 1 hour.

Mix the beef with the sun-dried tomatoes and mustard and season well with salt and pepper. Unwrap the butter and cut it into 4 equal-sized discs. Divide the beef mixture into 4 portions and mould each piece around a disc of butter. Cover and chill for 1 hour.

Heat a griddle pan or barbecue to hot. Brush the burgers with a little oil and cook them for about 5 minutes on each side, depending on how well you like them done.

To assemble, toast the buns on a hot griddle pan or barbecue and top each one with a garlic burger and salad leaves. Top with the lid and serve with the garlic mayonnaise.

beef steak burger with caramelized onions and straw parsnip chips

2 tablespoons light olive oil

3 onions, cut into thin segments

4 small rib-eye steaks

1 tablespoon cracked black pepper

2 tablespoons chopped thyme

To serve:

4 Soft Focaccia Rolls (*see page 85*)

1 bunch of watercress

1 quantity Horseradish Mayonnaise
  (*see page 93*)

1 quantity Straw Parsnip Chips with Thyme
  (*see page 82*)

Serves 4
Preparation time: 10 minutes
Cooking time: 35 minutes

Gently heat half the oil in a frying pan then add the onions. Cook over a low heat until the onions are caramelized, about 25 minutes. Set aside until needed.

Preheat a griddle pan or barbecue to hot. Lightly brush the steaks with the remaining oil and rub the pepper and thyme into the meat. Cook for about 4 minutes on each side, depending on how well you like them done.

To assemble, toast the rolls on a hot griddle pan or barbecue. Top the base of each roll with watercress leaves, a cooked steak and some of the caramelized onions. Drizzle with the Horseradish Mayonnaise and stack the parsnip chips on top. Serve the bun lid and extra watercress on the side.

the ultimate cheeseburger

625 g (1¼ lb) good quality minced beef

50 g (2 oz) quince paste, finely diced

2 tablespoons chopped parsley

1 tablespoon Dijon mustard

1 teaspoon cayenne pepper

1 tablespoon Worcestershire sauce

75 g (3 oz) Parmesan cheese, freshly
   grated

a little light olive oil

175 g (6 oz) mature Cheddar cheese, cut
   into thick slices

salt and pepper

To serve:

4 crusty rolls

salad leaves

1 beef tomato, sliced

a selection of pickles, such as gherkins and
   pickled onions

1 quantity Wholegrain Mustard Mayonnaise
   (see page 93)

Serves 4
Preparation time: 15 minutes, plus chilling
Cooking time: 15 minutes

Fresh quince has a flavour somewhere between an apple and a pear; because of its high pectin content it makes excellent jams and pastes. Quince paste is sweet with a delicate flowery taste and can be found on most cheese counters in large supermarkets.

Mix together the beef, quince paste, parsley, mustard, cayenne pepper, Worcestershire sauce and Parmesan in a large bowl. Season well with salt and pepper and divide into 4 portions. Form into balls and flatten slightly into burgers. Cover and chill for 30 minutes.

Heat a griddle pan to hot. Brush the burgers with a little oil and cook for about 5 minutes on each side, depending on how well you like them done. Divide the slices of cheese over the burgers and melt slightly under a hot grill.

To assemble, halve the rolls and toast under a grill and top each base with salad leaves and tomato slices followed by a burger and the lid. Serve immediately with a selection of pickles and wholegrain mustard mayonnaise on the side.

smoky beef burger with smoked mozzarella cheese

2 tablespoons olive oil, plus extra for
  brushing
1 onion, finely chopped
2 smoked or fresh garlic cloves, crushed
2 teaspoons smoked paprika
1 teaspoon cumin seeds, crushed
625 g (1¼ lb) good quality coarsely minced
  beef
200 g (7 oz) smoked bacon, finely chopped
125 g (4 oz) smoked mozzarella, cut into
  4 slices
salt and pepper

To serve:
4 crusty rolls
75 g (3 oz) mixed salad leaves
1 quantity Quick BBQ Sauce *(see page 92)*

Serves 4
Preparation time: 15 minutes, plus chilling
Cooking time: 20 minutes

Smoked garlic and smoked paprika can be bought in large supermarkets.

Heat 1 tablespoon of the oil in a frying pan and fry the onion, garlic, paprika and cumin seeds over a medium heat for 5 minutes until softened. Set aside to cool. Mix together the ground beef, onion mixture and smoked bacon. Season well with salt and pepper. Divide the mixture into 4 equal portions and form into balls then flatten slightly. Chill for at least 30 minutes.

Heat a griddle pan to medium-high. Brush the burgers with the remaining oil and cook for about 5 minutes on each side, depending on how well you like them done. Divide the slices of mozzarella between the burgers and melt slightly under a hot grill.

To assemble, halve and toast the rolls under a grill and top each base with salad leaves followed by a burger. Spoon over the quick BBQ sauce and serve topped with the lid of the roll.

fillet burger with a mustard and brandy cream sauce

625 g (1¼ lb) beef fillet

1 tablespoon light olive oil

25 g (1 oz) butter

3 shallots, finely chopped

1 garlic clove, chopped

2 tablespoons chopped thyme

2 tablespoons brandy

2 teaspoons Dijon mustard

125 ml (4 fl oz) crème fraîche

salt and pepper

To serve:

4 crusty rolls

rocket

Serves 4

Preparation time: 10 minutes

Cooking time: 10 minutes

Slice the beef fillet into 8 equal pieces and season with salt and pepper. Heat the oil in a frying pan and cook the beef slices for 2 minutes on each side. Remove the beef from the pan and set aside.

Melt the butter in the same pan and gently fry the shallots, garlic and thyme for 2–3 minutes or until soft. Pour in the brandy and bring to the boil. Stir in the mustard and crème fraîche then simmer for 2 minutes. Remove the pan from the heat then put the beef back into the pan to coat it in the sauce.

To assemble, halve and toast the rolls and top the base of each one with rocket and 2 slices of beef fillet. Spoon the remaining sauce over the burgers and serve immediately with the roll lid on the side.

aussie burger with the lot!

625 g (1¼ lb) good quality coarsely
   minced beef
2 garlic cloves, crushed
1 onion, finely chopped
1 tablespoon Dijon mustard
1 tablespoon Worcestershire sauce
1 tablespoon chopped thyme
4 back bacon rashers
4 small eggs
a little light olive oil, for cooking
salt and pepper

To serve:
4 burger buns
mixed salad leaves
8 slices of pickled beetroot, crinkle cut
4 thin slices Cheddar cheese
4 slices pineapple
1 quantity Southern Fried Onion Rings
   (see page 83)

Serves 4
Preparation time: 20 minutes, plus chilling
Cooking time: 20 minutes

Using crinkle cut beetroot or other crinkle cut pickles is an old trick in the making of burgers; it stops the pickles from sliding out of the bun while you are eating it. Simple yet effective.

Mix the beef, garlic, onion, mustard, Worcestershire sauce and thyme together in a bowl and season well. Divide the beef mixture into 4 equal portions and shape into balls then flatten into burgers. Cover and chill for 1 hour.

Grill the bacon until slightly crisp and keep it warm. Heat a griddle pan to medium-high. Brush the burgers with a little oil and cook them for about 5 minutes on each side, depending on how well you like them done.

Heat some oil in a frying pan and fry the eggs for 3–4 minutes or until the white part of the egg is cooked but the yolk is still soft. Meanwhile, halve and toast the buns under a grill.

To assemble, layer some salad leaves, the burger, bacon, Cheddar, pineapple, beetroot and egg on the base of each bun and top with the lid. Stick a skewer through the burger to prevent it falling apart and serve topped with the southern fried onion rings.

chilli-beef topped burger

500 g (1 lb) good quality minced beef

150 g (5 oz) pork and herb sausages,
  skinned

1 garlic clove, crushed

1 tablespoon Dijon mustard

2 tablespoons finely chopped parsley

a little light olive oil, for brushing

salt and pepper

Chilli sauce:

1 tablespoon light olive oil

1 onion, finely chopped

1 large red chilli, finely chopped

1 teaspoon paprika

1 garlic clove, crushed

200 g (7 oz) minced beef

450 ml (14½ fl oz) passata

1 tablespoon Worcestershire sauce

1 teaspoon Tabasco sauce

200 g (7 oz) can red kidney beans, drained
  and rinsed

To serve:

4 ciabatta rolls

salad leaves

Serves 4

Preparation time: 25 minutes, plus chilling

Cooking time: 35 minutes

First, make the chilli sauce. Heat the oil in a frying pan and cook the onion, chilli, paprika and garlic until soft, about 3–4 minutes. Add the minced beef and cook for 2–3 minutes until browned. Stir through the remaining sauce ingredients then season with salt and pepper and stir well. Cover and cook over a low heat for 20 minutes.

To make the burger, mix together the beef, sausage-meat, garlic, mustard and parsley in a bowl. Season well with salt and pepper and divide into 4 equal portions. Form into balls then flatten into burgers. Cover and chill for 30 minutes.

Heat a griddle pan or barbecue to hot. Brush the burgers with a little oil and cook for about 5 minutes on each side, depending on how well you like them done.

To assemble, halve the rolls and toast under a grill. Top each base with salad leaves followed by a burger. Spoon over the chilli sauce and serve with the roll lid on the side.

indian spiced burger with mango chutney

2 tablespoons light olive oil, plus extra
  for brushing

1 onion

2 garlic cloves, crushed

1 red chilli, deseeded and finely chopped

1 teaspoon black mustard seeds

1 tablespoon garam masala

1 teaspoon turmeric

625 g (1¼ lb) lamb mince

50 g (2 oz) breadcrumbs

1 small egg

salt and pepper

To serve:

8 mini naan breads

a small bunch of coriander, chopped

red chilli powder (optional)

½ cucumber, cubed

2 tomatoes, cubed

mango chutney

mini poppadums

Serves 4
Preparation time: 25 minutes, plus chilling
Cooking time: 15 minutes

Heat the oil in a frying pan and fry the onion, garlic, chilli, mustard seeds and spices for 5 minutes or until the onion has softened and the mustard seeds start to pop. Set aside to cool.

Mix together the lamb, breadcrumbs, egg and onion mixture in a large bowl. Season with salt and pepper then divide into 8 portions. Form them into round balls and flatten slightly into burgers. Cover and chill for at least 30 minutes.

Heat a griddle pan or barbecue to hot. Brush the burgers with a little oil and cook for 5 minutes on each side depending on how well you like them done.

To assemble, toast the naan breads on a hot griddle pan or barbecue until lightly browned. Top each naan with some coriander, a sprinkle of red chilli powder, if using, a burger and the cucumber and tomato. Serve with mango chutney and mini poppadums.

chermoula lamb burger
with slow-roasted tomatoes

625 g (1¼ lb) good quality coarsely
  minced lamb

75 g (3 oz) dried apricots, finely chopped

3 tablespoons finely chopped coriander

2 tablespoons finely chopped flat leaf
  parsley

2 garlic cloves, crushed

2 teaspoons ground cumin

½ teaspoon cayenne pepper

½ teaspoon turmeric

salt and pepper

Slow-roasted tomatoes:

6 medium Roma or plum tomatoes, halved

a large pinch of paprika

2 garlic cloves, chopped

1 tablespoon olive oil

salt and pepper

To serve:

4 Soft Rolls (*see page 85*)

salad leaves

Serves 4
Preparation time: 12 minutes, plus chilling
Cooking time: 1¼ hours

Chermoula is traditionally used in Moroccan cooking as a marinade for fish but the strong flavours go especially well with this lamb burger.

Place the tomatoes cut side up on a lightly greased nonstick baking sheet. Sprinkle over the paprika and chopped garlic and season well with salt and pepper. Drizzle with olive oil and roast in a preheated oven, 150°C (300°F) Gas Mark 2, for 1 hour. Remove and set aside until needed.

Mix all the burger ingredients in a large bowl and season well with salt and pepper. Divide into 4 equal portions; form them into balls and flatten into burgers. Cover and chill for 30 minutes.

Heat a griddle pan or barbecue to hot. Brush the burgers with a little oil and cook them for 5 minutes on each side depending on how well you like them done.

To assemble, toast the halved rolls on a hot griddle pan or barbecue and top each base with salad leaves and a burger. Place 3 roasted tomatoes on each burger and top with the lid of the roll.

greek-style lamb burger

625 g (1¼ lb) good quality coarsely
   minced lamb
2 garlic cloves, crushed
grated rind of 1 lemon
150 g (5 oz) feta cheese, diced
50 g (2 oz) black olives, chopped
50 g (2 oz) pine nuts, dry-roasted and
   chopped
3 tablespoons chopped oregano

Salad:
3 tomatoes, cut into wedges
½ cucumber, cut into ribbons with a
   vegetable peeler
50 g (2 oz) Kalamata olives
1 tablespoon chopped flat leaf parsley

To serve:
4 floured rolls
pine nuts
Greek yogurt
lemon wedges

Serves 4
Preparation time: 20 minutes, plus chilling
Cooking time: 10 minutes

Mix together all the ingredients for the burger in a bowl and season well. Divide the mix into 4 equal portions and form into balls then flatten slightly into burgers. Cover and chill for at least 30 minutes.

Heat a griddle pan or barbecue to hot. Brush the burgers with a little oil and cook for about 5 minutes on each side, depending on how well you like them done.

Halve the rolls and toast under a grill. Top each base with some salad, the burgers and pine nuts and serve with Greek yogurt and lemon wedges.

lamb fillet burger

4 lamb leg steaks, about 150 g (5 oz) each

1 small aubergine, cut into 8 slices

Marinade:

3 teaspoons ground cumin

2 teaspoons ground coriander

2 garlic cloves, crushed

2 tablespoons finely chopped mint

grated rind of 1 lemon

75 ml (3 oz) olive oil

salt and pepper

Mint dressing:

125 ml (4 fl oz) Greek yogurt

1 garlic clove, crushed

2 tablespoons chopped mint

juice of 1 lemon

To serve:

4 burger buns

salad leaves

Serves 4

Preparation time: 20 minutes, plus
  marinating

Cooking time: 8 minutes

First marinate the lamb and aubergines. Mix together all the marinade ingredients, season well with salt and pepper and pour over the lamb steaks and aubergine slices. Cover and leave to marinate for 1 hour.

Heat a griddle pan or barbecue to medium or use a heavy-based frying pan. Add the steaks and aubergine slices and cook for 4 minutes on each side depending on how well you like them done. Brush with the remaining marinade during cooking.

To make the mint dressing, mix together all the ingredients and season to taste with salt and pepper.

To assemble, halve and lightly toast the buns and then top each base with salad leaves, 2 aubergine slices, more leaves then a lamb steak. Drizzle with the mint dressing and top with the bun lid.

jerk pork burger with mango salsa

625 g (1¼ lb) good quality, coarsely
  minced pork

2 tablespoon jerk seasoning

grated rind of 1 lime

2.5 cm (1 inch) piece of fresh root ginger,
  grated

2 garlic cloves, crushed

4 spring onions, finely chopped

1 tablespoon thyme

Mango salsa:

1 mango, peeled, cored and finely diced

½ red onion, peeled, finely diced

1 red chilli, deseeded and finely diced

2 tablespoons chopped mint

1 tablespoon chopped coriander

2 tablespoons olive oil

grated rind and juice of 1 lime

To serve:

4 burger buns

salad leaves

4 large pieces of marinated roasted
  red pepper

1 quantity Cajun Sweet Potato Chips
  (see page 80)

Serves 4
Preparation time: 25 minutes, plus chilling
Cooking time: 10 minutes

Marinated roasted peppers are available in deli sections at most supermarkets or they can be bought, preserved, in jars.

Mix together all the ingredients for the burger in a large bowl. Season well with salt and pepper then divide into 4 equal portions. Shape into balls and flatten slightly into burgers. Cover and chill for 30 minutes.

To make the salsa, mix together all the ingredients and set aside for at least 30 minutes at room temperature to allow the flavours to develop.

Heat a griddle pan or barbecue to hot. Brush the burgers with a little oil and cook them for 5 minutes on each side depending on how well you like them done.

To assemble, cut the buns in half and toast lightly on the griddle pan or barbecue. Top each base with salad leaves, roasted pepper and a burger. Spoon over the salsa and top with the lid. Serve with the Cajun sweet potato chips.

english breakfast burger

500 g (1 lb) good quality thick pork
  sausages
3 tablespoons chopped chives
1 teaspoon English mustard powder
a little light olive oil, for frying
a little flour, to dust
salt and pepper

To serve:
4 muffins
8 bacon rashers
4 slices of black pudding or blood sausage
  (optional)
4 free-range eggs
a little light olive oil, for frying
1 quantity Tomato Ketchup (*see page 92*)

Serves 4
Preparation time: 20 minutes
Cooking time: 20 minutes

This is the ultimate breakfast on the go. It's great served with English breakfast tea.

Remove the skins from the sausages and discard. Place the meat in a bowl with the chives and mustard powder. With floured hands, divide and shape the mixture into 4 thin burgers.

Cook the bacon and black pudding, if using, under a preheated grill until cooked through and slightly crisp, about 5 minutes. Set aside and keep warm.

Heat a little oil in a nonstick frying pan and cook the sausage burgers for 4 minutes on each side or until cooked through and golden brown. Remove from the pan and drain on kitchen paper.

In the same pan, add a little more oil and fry the eggs for 3–4 minutes or until the white is cooked but the yolk is soft.

To assemble, layer the burger, bacon, black pudding and egg between halved toasted muffins. Serve with tomato ketchup.

pork, leek and apple burger

25 g (1 oz) butter

1 medium leek, finely chopped

1 cooking apple, peeled and grated

2 garlic cloves, crushed

1 teaspoon mace

1 tablespoon chopped rosemary

625 g (1¼ lb) pork mince

a little oil, for brushing

salt and pepper

Apple balsamic relish:

2 apples, chopped

250 g (8 oz) baby plum tomatoes

1 red onion, chopped

2 garlic cloves, chopped

1 tablespoon green peppercorns

3 sprigs of thyme

1 teaspoon rock salt

50 g (2 oz) sugar

50 ml (2 fl oz) balsamic vinegar

200 ml (7 fl oz) apple cider

To serve:

4 crusty rolls

salad leaves

1 red onion, thinly sliced into rings

Serves 4
Preparation time: 20 minutes, plus chilling
Cooking time: 10 minutes

Melt the butter in a frying pan and fry the leek, apple, garlic and mace over a medium heat for 4–5 minutes until tender. Add the rosemary and leave to cool. Mix together the minced pork and the leek mixture and season well with salt and pepper. Divide the mixture into 4 equal portions, form each one into a ball, then flatten slightly to make a burger. Cover and chill for at least 30 minutes.

Meanwhile, make the apple balsamic relish. Place all the ingredients into a large heavy-based pan and gently bring to the boil. Simmer over a medium heat for 25 minutes, stirring occasionally until thick.

Heat a griddle pan or barbecue to hot. Brush the burgers with a little oil and cook for 5 minutes on each side or until they are cooked through.

To assemble, halve the rolls and toast lightly under a grill. Fill with lots of salad leaves, onion and the burger. Top with spoonfuls of apple balsamic relish and serve immediately.

maple syrup glazed pork fillet burger
with roasted pears

25 g (1 oz) butter

2 pears, cut into segments

6 tablespoons maple syrup

1 tablespoon red wine vinegar

1 tablespoon wholegrain mustard

2 teaspoons grated ginger

1 tablespoon chopped sage leaves

2 tablespoons olive oil

4 pork loin medallions, about 125 g
   (4 oz) each

salt and pepper

To serve:

4 soft rolls

salad leaves

Serves 4

Preparation time: 5 minutes

Cooking time: 20 minutes

Heat the butter in a frying pan, add the pears and fry until lightly browned. Add 2 tablespoons of the maple syrup and cook until lightly caramelized. Transfer to a roasting dish and baked in a preheated oven, 200°C (400°F) Gas Mark 6, for 10 minutes or until cooked though. Keep warm until needed.

In a small bowl, whisk together the remaining maple syrup, with the vinegar, mustard, ginger, sage and a little salt and pepper until well combined.

Heat the olive oil in a large frying pan over medium-high heat. Add the pork fillets and cook for 4 minutes on each side or until browned and just cooked through. Pour the maple syrup mixture over the pork and turn to coat the meat in the sauce and cook for 1 further minute.

To assemble, halve the rolls and toast under a grill. Fill each one with salad leaves, a pork steak and some of the baked pears. Serve immediately.

pork sausage burger with potato rosti and balsamic roasted onions

200 g (7 oz) rindless pork belly, chopped

400 g (14 oz) pork mince

2 teaspoons mace

2 tablespoons chopped rosemary

½ teaspoon cayenne pepper

grated rind of 1 lemon

a little oil, for brushing

salt and pepper

Potato rosti:

2 potatoes, peeled and coarsely grated

2 garlic cloves, crushed

2 tablespoons light olive oil

25 g (1 oz) unsalted butter

Roasted balsamic onions:

2 red onions, cut into quarters

a dash of olive oil

2 tablespoons balsamic vinegar

a few sprigs of thyme

To serve:

mixed salad leaves

a small bunch of rosemary

Serves 4

Preparation time: 20 minutes, plus chilling

Cooking time: 55 minutes

To make the burgers, place the pork belly in a food processor and blitz until finely chopped. Combine this with the pork mince, mace, rosemary and cayenne pepper and season well with salt and pepper. Divide into 4 equal portions and shape each one into a ball. Flatten slightly to make a burger then cover and chill for 30 minutes.

Next, cook the roasted onions. Toss the red onions with a dash of olive oil and the balsamic vinegar in a roasting tin. Sprinkle with the thyme and cook in a preheated oven, 190°C (375°F) Gas Mark 5, for 30 minutes or until slightly charred around the edges.

Meanwhile, begin making the potato rosti. When the onions are done, turn the oven up to 220°C (425°F) Gas Mark 7. Place the grated potato on a clean tea towel and squeeze out any excess moisture. Transfer to a bowl and add the garlic. Mix thoroughly and season well with salt and pepper. Divide the mixture into 4 portions and shape into flat discs. Heat the oil and butter in a pan and fry the rostis for 2 minutes on each side or until lightly browed. Transfer to an ovenproof dish and bake in the preheated oven until crisp, about 10 minutes.

Heat a griddle pan or barbecue to medium-high. Brush the burgers with a little oil and cook for 5 minutes on each side or until they are cooked through.

To assemble, place the salad leaves on the potato rostis and top with a burger, a spoonful of roasted onions and a sprig of rosemary.

poultry

turkey and chestnut burger
with cranberry and brie

1 tablespoon olive oil

1 onion, chopped

2 garlic cloves, crushed

50 g (2 oz) chestnuts, roughly chopped

2 tablespoons chopped thyme

625 g (1¼ lb) coarsely minced turkey

50 g (2 oz) fresh breadcrumbs

1 egg

1 tablespoon cranberry sauce

a little light olive oil, for brushing

salt and pepper

To serve:

4 burger buns

125 g (4 oz) Brie cheese

4 tablespoons cranberry sauce

salad leaves

Serves 4
Preparation time: 15 minutes, plus chilling
Cooking time: 16 minutes

Heat the oil in a pan and fry the onion and garlic for 4 minutes or until the onion has softened. Remove from the heat and add the chestnuts and thyme. Set aside to cool.

Put the turkey, breadcrumbs, egg, cranberry sauce, chestnuts, thyme and onion mixture in a large bowl. Season with salt and pepper and mix well. Divide into 4 equal portions and form each one into a round ball. Flatten slightly into burgers then cover and chill for at least 30 minutes.

Heat a griddle pan to medium-high. Brush the burgers with a little oil and cook for 6 minutes on each side or until cooked through.

Slice the Brie into 4 pieces and place one on each burger. Melt under a hot grill then put each one in a toasted bun and top with cranberry sauce. Serve with salad leaves.

chicken satay burger

300 g (10 oz) skinless, boneless chicken
   breast, chopped

300 g (10 oz) skinless, boneless chicken
   thighs, chopped

2 teaspoons harissa

1 red onion, finely chopped

4 tablespoons chopped coriander

50 g (2 oz) fresh breadcrumbs

1 egg yolk

salt and pepper

Satay sauce:

200 ml (7 fl oz) crunchy peanut butter

250 ml (8 fl oz) coconut milk

2 tablespoons soy sauce

1 red chilli, finely chopped

2.5 cm (1 inch) piece of fresh root ginger,
   peeled and grated

2 garlic cloves, crushed

juice and grated rind of 1 lime

2 tablespoons sweet chilli sauce

To serve:

½ cucumber, cut into ribbons with a
   vegetable peeler

a small bunch of coriander

1 lime, cut into wedges

Serves 4
Preparation time: 20 minutes, plus chilling
Cooking time: 10 minutes

This is perfect as a starter for 6 people or as a hot canapé. For a main course, serve with a crusty roll and extra salad.

First mix together all the ingredients for the satay sauce in a small saucepan. Bring to the boil and simmer, stirring continuously, for 2 minutes. Remove from the heat and set aside until needed.

Mix together all the ingredients for the burger. Divide the mixture into 12 pieces and shape into balls then flatten slightly to make burgers. Cover and chill for at least 30 minutes.

Heat a griddle pan or barbecue to medium. Brush the burgers with a little oil and cook for about 4 minutes on each side or until cooked through.

Serve the mini burgers accompanied by a bowl of the satay sauce for dipping. Garnish the burgers with ribbons of cucumber, coriander sprigs and wedges of lime.

teriyaki chicken burger with japanese mayo and crisp salad

4 skinless, boneless chicken breasts, about
 150–175 g (5–6 oz) each
2 tablespoons sesame seeds
1 tablespoon olive oil, plus extra for
 greasing
salt and pepper

Teriyaki marinade:
75 ml (3 fl oz) sake
1 tablespoon clear honey
50 ml (2 fl oz) light soy sauce
2.5 cm (1 inch) piece of fresh root ginger,
 peeled and finely grated
1 garlic clove, finely grated

To serve:
4 Soft Rolls (*see page 85*)
¼ cucumber, thinly sliced
Cos lettuce, shredded
3 spring onions, shredded
2 chopped tablespoons coriander
Japanese mayonnaise (can be found in
 most Asian stores)

Serves 4
**Preparation time: 25 minutes, plus cooling
 and marinating**
Cooking time: 20 minutes

First make the marinade. Put all the marinade ingredients in a small pan and boil for 2 minutes. Remove from the heat and leave to cool.

Next, prepare the burgers. Slice each chicken breast in half on a slight angle so you have 8 equal slices. Score each slice a few times with a sharp knife and pour over the marinade. Season with salt and pepper then cover and chill for 1 hour.

Place the chicken slices on a lightly greased grill pan and sprinkle with half the sesame seeds. Drizzle with the oil and cook under a preheated hot grill for 8 minutes. Turn the chicken, sprinkle with the remaining sesame seeds and cook for a further 8 minutes, spooning over the cooking juices to baste the meat.

To assemble, halve and toast the rolls. Place a little cucumber on the base of each one, then add 2 slices of chicken. Mix together the lettuce, spring onion and coriander and divide equally over the chicken slices. Top with the lid and serve with Japanese mayo.

chicken caesar burger

500 g (1 lb) coarsely minced chicken breast

2 garlic cloves, crushed

1 bunch of spring onions, finely chopped

grated rind of 1 lemon

50 g (2 oz) Parmesan cheese, freshly
  grated

2 anchovies, chopped

8 streaky bacon rashers

salt and pepper

To serve:

1 tablespoon olive oil

4 small French baguettes, cut in half
  lengthways

1 small Cos lettuce, separated into leaves

Caesar salad dressing

Parmesan cheese shavings

Serves 4

Preparation time: 25 minutes, plus chilling

Cooking time: 10 minutes

You can buy good Caesar dressing these days, so there's no need to make
your own. Get the best quality you can, though.

Mix together all the ingredients for the burger, except the bacon, in a bowl
and season with salt and pepper. Divide the mixture into 4 balls and flatten
slightly into burgers. Wrap each one in 2 rashers of bacon then cover and
chill for at least 30 minutes.

Heat a griddle pan or barbecue to medium. Brush the burgers with a
little oil and cook them for about 5 minutes on each side or until
cooked through.

To assemble, brush the insides of the baguettes with oil and toast under a
hot grill until golden. Top each one with lettuce leaves and drizzle with
some dressing. Place a burger on the salad and top with shaved Parmesan.

crunchy chicken burger with ham and cheese

4 small chicken breasts, about 150–175 g
   (5–6 oz) each

125 g (4 oz) breadcrumbs

grated rind of 1 lemon

2 tablespoons chopped parsley

1 large chilli, deseeded and finely chopped

1 tablespoon wholegrain mustard

1 egg, beaten

2 tablespoons olive oil

25 g (1 oz) butter

4 slices of Jarlsburg or Edam cheese,
   about 25 g (1 oz) each

To serve:

4 burger buns

125 g (4 oz) mixed salad leaves

4 thin slices of ham

mayonnaise

Serves 4
Preparation time: 15 minutes
Cooking time: 10 minutes

Place each chicken breast between 2 sheets of clingfilm and beat until thin with a meat mallet or rolling pin. Mix together the breadcrumbs, lemon rind, parsley and chilli and sprinkle on a large plate. Spread the mustard over the chicken escalopes then dip them first in the beaten egg and then the breadcrumbs.

Heat the oil and butter in a frying pan and fry the chicken over a medium heat until golden and cooked through, about 4 minutes on each side. Arrange the sliced cheese over the chicken and cook under a hot grill until the cheese starts to bubble.

Slice open the baps or burger buns and fill with salad, chicken and sliced ham. Serve with a dollop of mayonnaise on the side.

thai chicken burger with sweet chilli sauce

550 g (1 lb 2 oz) coarsely minced chicken

1 onion, finely chopped

2 garlic cloves, crushed

grated rind of 1 lime

3 tablespoons chopped Thai or
  ordinary basil

3 tablespoon red Thai curry paste

a little oil, for brushing

To serve:

4 Crusty Sesame Seed Rolls (*see page 84*)

a little olive oil, for stir-frying

4 heads of bok choi, sliced lengthways

6 tablespoons sweet chilli sauce

basil leaves

Serves 4

Preparation time: 20 minutes, plus chilling

Cooking time: 10 minutes

Mix together all the ingredients for the burgers. Divide into 4 portions and shape into balls then flatten slightly to make burgers Cover and chill for at least 30 minutes.

Brush the burgers with a little oil and cook them in a frying pan over a medium heat for about 5 minutes on each side or until cooked through.

Heat the oil and stir-fry the bok choi for 2 minutes or until just cooked. Toast the rolls under a grill until golden. Put some bok choi on the base of each roll then add a burger. Drizzle with sweet chilli sauce and garnish with extra basil leaves. Place the lid on top or to the side and serve.

sticky lemongrass and ginger chicken burger

200 g (7 oz) skinless, boneless chicken
  breast, chopped

400 g (13 oz) skinless, boneless chicken
  thigh, chopped

1 bunch of spring onions, finely chopped

2 tablespoons lemon grass purée

1 inch (2.5 cm) piece of fresh root
  ginger, peeled and grated

2 garlic cloves, crushed

3 tablespoons chopped coriander

2 tablespoons light olive oil

1 tablespoon dark soy sauce

1 tablespoon fish sauce

1 tablespoon rice wine vinegar

1 tablespoon water

2 tablespoons caster sugar

To serve:

4 Crusty Chilli Flake Rolls (*see page 84*)

4 spring onions, shredded

¼ cucumber, cut into thin sticks

8 large basil leaves

8 large mint leaves

a small bunch of coriander

4 lime wedges

Serves 4
Preparation time: 20 minutes, plus chilling
Cooking time: 10 minutes

Puréed lemon grass gives this dish a wonderful flavour and is well worth seeking out. It can be bought in jars from Asian supermarkets.

Place all the chicken thigh and breast meat in a food processor and blitz until roughly chopped. Add the spring onion, lemon grass, ginger, garlic and coriander then blitz for a further 2 seconds until combined. Divide the mixture into 4 and form into burgers. Cover and chill for 30 minutes.

Heat the oil in a shallow frying pan and fry the burgers for 4 minutes on each side until golden and slightly crisp. Add the soy sauce, fish sauce, vinegar, water and sugar and stir until the sugar dissolves. Cover with a lid and cook for a further 3 minutes, turning the burgers occasionally, until the sauce is slightly sticky and the chicken is cooked through.

To assemble, halve the rolls and toast. Cover each base with onions, cucumber and herbs then place a sticky chicken burger on top. Serve with wedges of lime and the lid on the side.

roast chicken burger with sage and onion stuffing

4 small chicken breasts, skin on

2 garlic cloves, crushed

2 tablespoons chopped flat leaf parsley

1 tablespoon olive oil

salt and pepper

Sage and onion stuffing:

1 tablespoon light olive oil, plus extra for
    greasing

1 onion, finely chopped

4 pork sausages

4 tablespoons chopped sage

125 g (4 oz) fresh breadcrumbs

1 egg, beaten

To serve:

4 crusty rolls

Iceberg lettuce, shredded

Serves 4
Preparation time: 25 minutes
Cooking time: 40 minutes

First make the stuffing. Heat the oil in a frying pan and cook the onion until soft but not coloured, about 4 minutes. Remove from the heat and allow to cool slightly. Remove the skins from the sausages and mix the meat with the cooked onion, sage, breadcrumbs and egg. Divide the mixture into 8 pieces, shape them into 8 burger-shaped rounds and place in a lightly greased roasting tin.

Mix together the garlic, parsley and olive oil and brush over the chicken breasts. Place them in a roasting tin and season well with salt and pepper.

Roast both the stuffing and chicken in a preheated oven, 200°C (400°F) Gas Mark 6, for 35 minutes or until golden brown and cooked through.

To assemble, halve the rolls and toast under a grill. Top each base with shredded lettuce then 2 stuffing burgers and a roasted chicken breast. Serve immediately with the lid on the side.

wild mushroom chicken burger with tarragon

400 g (13 oz) skinless, boneless chicken
  thigh, roughly chopped
200 g (7 oz) skinless boneless chicken
  breast, roughly chopped
1 onion, finely chopped
2 garlic cloves, crushed
3 tablespoons chopped tarragon
1 tablespoon Dijon mustard
a little light olive oil, for frying

Mushroom sauce:
25 g (1 oz) butter
250 g (8 oz) mixed wild mushrooms,
  roughly chopped
1 teaspoon wholegrain mustard
1 tablespoon red wine vinegar
125 ml (4 oz) crème fraîche

To serve:
4 crusty rolls
50 g (2 oz) wild rocket

Serves 4
Preparation time: 15 minutes, plus chilling
Cooking time: 20 minutes

This wonderfully tasty burger is really enhanced by the flavour of the wild mushrooms so don't stint on them – use more if you think the sauce needs them.

Place the chicken thigh and breast meat in a food processor and blitz until roughly chopped. Add the onion, garlic, tarragon and mustard and blitz for a further 2 seconds until combined. Divide the mixture into 4 portions and shape into burgers. Cover and chill for 30 minutes.

Heat the oil in a frying pan and fry the burgers over a medium heat for 6 minutes on each side or until golden and slightly crisp. Remove the burgers from the pan and keep them warm.

Melt the butter in the same pan and gently cook the mushrooms for 4–5 minutes until cooked. Stir in the mustard, vinegar and crème fraîche and cook for 1–2 minutes or until the sauce is thick enough to coat the back of a spoon.

To assemble, halve the rolls and toast lightly then top each base with rocket followed by a burger. Spoon the wild mushroom sauce over the top and serve with the bun lid on the side.

chicken and goat's cheese burger

4 skinless chicken breasts

2 tablespoons chopped thyme

2 garlic cloves, crushed

4 thin slices Parma ham

150 g (5 oz) goat's cheese

a little light olive oil, for brushing

salt and pepper

Honey-roasted figs:

6 figs, cut into quarters

2 tablespoons olive oil

2 tablespoons clear orange
  blossom honey

salt and pepper

To serve:

4 Crusty Caraway Seed Rolls (*see page 84*)

75 g (3 oz) rocket or thyme sprigs

Serves 4

Preparation time: 15 minutes

Cooking time: 17 minutes

Make sure you get goat's cheese with a rind, rather than the packaged soft cheese that's often available. The cheese with a rind has a richer flavour and will melt more pleasingly over the burger.

First, cook the honey-roasted figs. Place the figs in a roasting dish and drizzle with the olive oil and honey. Season well with salt and pepper and roast in a preheated oven, 200°C (400°F) Gas Mark 6, for 10 minutes until the figs just start to colour.

Meanwhile, sandwich each chicken breast between 2 sheets of clingfilm and flatten slightly with a rolling pin or meat mallet. Rub the thyme and garlic into the chicken, season with salt and pepper and wrap with the Parma ham.

Heat a griddle pan or barbecue to medium. Brush the chicken with oil and cook for about 8 minutes on each side or until cooked through. Top each breast with a slice of goat's cheese and melt slightly under a hot grill.

To assemble, halve the rolls and toast under a grill, top each base with rocket leaves and a chicken breast. Spoon the honey-roasted figs over each burger and garnish with extra rocket leaves or thyme sprigs and serve the lids on the side.

fish

parmesan-crusted cod burger
with lemon mayo

1 egg

1 teaspoon English mustard powder

75 g (3 oz) fresh breadcrumbs

2 tablespoons finely chopped basil

25 g (1 oz) Parmesan cheese, freshly
  grated

4 tablespoons plain flour

4 cod fillets, about 175 g (6 oz) each

2 tablespoons light olive oil

salt and pepper

To serve:

4 Crusty Poppy Seed Rolls (*see page 84*)

mixed salad leaves

1 beef tomato, sliced

4 tablespoons Lemon Mayonnaise (*see
  page 93*)

lemon wedges

Serves 4

Preparation time: 15 minutes

Cooking time: 8 minutes

First make the crust for the fish. Beat the egg and mustard with a little salt and pepper. Mix together the breadcrumbs, basil and Parmesan in a bowl then turn out on to a plate. Spread the flour on a separate plate.

Coat the cod fillets in the flour and dip them first in the egg mixture then coat evenly in the breadcrumb mixture.

Heat the oil in a shallow pan and fry the fish until golden and cooked through, about 4 minutes on each side.

Halve the rolls and toast under a grill then fill with the salad leaves, tomato slices and crusted cod fillets. Serve with the lids on the side and lemon mayonnaise, lemon wedges and extra salad.

swordfish steak burger with crunchy orange salsa

1 teaspoon ground cumin

1 teaspoon ground coriander

1 teaspoon paprika

a pinch of ground chilli

grated rind of 1 orange

2 tablespoons olive oil

4 swordfish steaks, about 175 g (6 oz) each

salt and pepper

Crunchy orange salsa:

1 large orange, segmented and finely
  chopped

3 tablespoons finely chopped flat leaf
  parsley

1 red chilli, finely chopped

3 spring onions, finely chopped

3 tablespoons olive oil

3 garlic cloves, finely sliced

2.5 cm (1 inch) piece of fresh root ginger,
  peeled and cut into fine matchsticks

1 teaspoon cumin seeds

To serve:

4 Crusty Sesame Seed Rolls (*see page 84*)

mixed salad leaves

Serves 4

Preparation time: 20 minutes

Cooking time: 10 minutes

First make the salsa by mixing together the orange, parsley, chilli and spring onions in a bowl. Heat the oil in a frying pan and cook the garlic, ginger and cumin seeds until crisp. Add the contents of the pan to the orange mixture and stir. Set aside until needed.

To make the burger, mix together the spices, orange rind and oil, season with salt and pepper and rub over both sides of the swordfish steaks. Heat a griddle pan or barbecue to medium-high and cook the steaks for 8–10 minutes, turning once, until cooked through.

To assemble, place salad leaves on the base of the rolls and put the fish steaks on top. Spoon over the orange salsa and top with the bun lid.

pan-fried salmon burger with minted pea salsa

500 g (1 lb) salmon fillet, skinned

4 spring onions, finely chopped

1 courgette, roughly grated

50 g (2 oz) breadcrumbs

1 egg yolk

a little oil, for frying

Minted pea salsa:

200 g (7 oz) frozen peas

½ red onion, finely chopped

3 tablespoons chopped mint

juice of 1 lime

2 tablespoons olive oil

To serve:

4 crusty rolls

50 g (2 oz) baby spinach leaves

1 beef tomato, sliced

Serves 4

Preparation time: 20 minutes, plus chilling

Cooking time: 10 minutes

First, make the salsa. Put the peas into a pan of boiling water, bring back to the boil then drain and refresh under cold running water. Blitz in a food processor until finely chopped. Put the chopped peas in a bowl and stir in the rest of the salsa ingredients. Set aside until needed.

To make the burger, blitz the salmon fillet in a food processor until finely chopped. Add the remaining burger ingredients and blitz until just mixed but not puréed. With slightly wet hands, divide the mixture into 4 equal portions and form into burgers. Cover and chill for 30 minutes.

Heat the oil in a shallow pan and fry the burgers over a medium heat for 4 minutes on each side, until golden brown and cooked through.

Halve the rolls and toast under the grill then fill with the baby spinach, tomato slices and the burgers. Top each burger with some minted pea salsa and serve with the lid on the side.

sesame salmon burger

8 tablespoons sesame seeds

4 tablespoons black sesame seeds

4 salmon fillets, about 150 g (5 oz) each,
 skinned

2 tablespoons olive oil

1 tablespoon roasted sesame oil

To serve:

2 Crusty Sesame Seed Rolls (*see page 84*)

½ cucumber, cut into ribbons with a
 vegetable peeler

1 small red onion, finely sliced

Serves 4

Preparation time: 10 minutes

Cooking time: 8 minutes

The black sesame seeds give a real professional restaurant look to this burger; you can buy them in most Japanese or Indian stores.

Spread the sesame seeds on a large plate then dip in the salmon fillets so the top side of each is evenly coated. Heat the oil in a shallow pan and fry the salmon over a medium heat for 4 minutes on each side or until golden and cooked through. Remove from the heat and drizzle over the roasted sesame oil.

Halve the rolls and toast under a grill. Top each half with some cucumber and red onion. Top with a salmon burger and serve immediately with extra salad.

tuna steak with wasabi mayo

3 shallots, thinly sliced

2.5 cm (1 inch) piece of fresh root
  ginger, grated

1 garlic clove, crushed

1 tablespoon clear honey

4 tablespoons Japanese soy sauce

2 tablespoons rice wine vinegar

4 tuna steaks, about 200 g (7 oz) each

2 tablespoons olive oil

Wasabi mayo:

8 tablespoons mayonnaise

1–2 teaspoons wasabi

To serve:

4 burger buns

¼ cucumber, shredded

frisée lettuce leaves

8 large mint leaves, shredded

Serves 4

**Preparation time: 10 minutes, plus
  marinating**

Cooking time: 8 minutes

Wasabi is a Japanese horseradish with a sharp, fiery and pungent flavour. You can buy it in dried and paste form from most Asian stores.

***

To make the wasabi mayo, simply mix together the two ingredients and chill until needed.

Make a marinade by stirring together the shallots, ginger, garlic, honey, soy sauce and vinegar. Put the tuna into a non-metallic bowl and pour over the marinade. Cover and leave for 1 hour but no more or the vinegar in the marinade will start to cook the fish.

Heat a griddle pan or barbecue to hot. Remove the tuna steaks from the marinade and lightly brush with the olive oil. Cook for 3–4 minutes on each side spooning over the marinade to baste the fish.

To assemble, halve the buns and toast on the barbecue or under a grill. Top each base with some frisée and mint then put a tuna steak on top. Add the bun lid and serve with a dollop of wasabi mayo on the side.

cajun fish burger

625 g (1¼ lb) white fish fillet

50 g (2 oz) fresh breadcrumbs

1 small onion, grated

1 garlic clove

1 egg yolk

1 teaspoon Tabasco sauce

a little light olive oil, for frying

Cajun spice mix:

3 teaspoons paprika

1 teaspoon cayenne pepper

1 teaspoon dried thyme

1 teaspoon dried parsley

1 teaspoon dried oregano

½ teaspoon onion salt

a pinch of cinnamon

To serve:

4 crusty rolls

salad leaves

1 quantity Butter Bean, Tomato and
   Coriander Salsa (*see page 95*)

Serves 4
Preparation time: 15 minutes, plus chilling
Cooking time: 10 minutes

Heat a small frying pan and add all the ingredients for the Cajun spice mix, cook for 1 minute until the spices start to smoke slightly. This will enhance their flavours. Set aside to cool.

Skin and bone the fish then chop roughly. Put it in a food processor with the breadcrumbs, onion, garlic, egg, Tabasco and spice mix and blitz until thoroughly blended and the mixture holds together. Don't overblend as you want the fish to have some texture.

With slightly wet hands, divide the mixture into 4 equal portions; shape them into balls then flatten into burgers. Cover and chill for 1 hour.

Heat the oil in a shallow pan and fry the burgers over a medium-high heat for 5 minutes on each side or until golden and cooked through.

To assemble, halve the rolls and toast under a grill. Place a little salad on the base and top with a burger. Spoon over some of the salsa and serve immediately with the lid on the side.

beer-battered fish burger

100 g (3½ oz) plain flour

a pinch of baking powder

200 ml (7 fl oz) lager

vegetable oil, for deep frying

4 cod fillets, about 175 g (6 oz) each

salt and pepper

To serve:

4 crusty rolls

a little butter, for spreading

salad leaves

1 quantity Tomato Ketchup (*see page 92*)

1 quantity Mixed Herb Mayonnaise (*see page 93*)

home-made chips (optional)

Serves 4

Preparation time: 15 minutes, plus chilling

Cooking time: 5 minutes

Although it's delicious, if you don't have the time to make your own ketchup, the bought variety is fine for this recipe.

To make the batter, whisk together the flour, baking powder and beer to make a smooth batter. Season with salt and pepper and leave to rest in the refrigerator for 20 minutes.

Half-fill a large pan or deep-fat fryer with the oil and heat to 180°C (350°F) or until a cube of bread browns in 30 seconds.

Dip the cod fillets into the batter, shake off any excess and cook in the oil for 5 minutes or until golden brown and cooked through. (You may need to do this in 2 batches or more depending on the size of your pan. Never over-fill a pan of hot oil.) Drain on plenty of kitchen paper.

To assemble, halve and butter the crusty rolls. Fill with salad leaves and the battered fish. Top with the mixed herb mayonnaise and serve with tomato ketchup and home-made chips (optional).

crab cake burgers with sweetcorn salsa

425 g (14 oz) fresh white crab meat

1 egg, beaten

2 tablespoons mayonnaise

a good pinch of English mustard powder

2 tablespoons lemon juice

½ red onion, grated

3 tablespoon chives, chopped

a few drops of Tabasco sauce

150 g (5 oz) fresh breadcrumbs

a little oil, for frying

salt and pepper

Sweetcorn salsa:

125 g (4 oz) frozen sweetcorn kernels

1 small red onion, finely chopped

1 avocado, finely chopped

2 tablespoons chopped chives

1 tablespoon red wine vinegar

2 tablespoons olive oil

To serve:

4 Soft Rolls (*see page 85*)

salad leaves

Serves 4

Preparation time: 20 minutes, plus chilling

Cooking time: 10 minutes

In a bowl, combine all the ingredients for the burger, except the breadcrumbs, and season lightly with salt and pepper. Divide into 4 equal burgers. Spread the breadcrumbs on a plate and coat each burger in them evenly. The mix is very wet so you may need to reshape the burgers in the crumbs. Cover and chill for 1 hour.

To make the salsa, boil the sweetcorn for 2 minutes then drain and refresh under cold running water. Place the sweetcorn in a bowl with the red onion, avocado, chives, vinegar and oil. Season well with salt and pepper and mix thoroughly. Set aside until needed.

Heat the oil in a shallow pan and fry the burgers for 2–3 minutes on each side or until heated through and crisp. Drain on kitchen paper.

To assemble, halve the rolls and toast under a grill. Top each base with a little salad and a burger. Serve with the salsa and the lid on the side.

polenta-crusted prawn burgers with harissa dressing

150 g (5 oz) white fish

425 g (14 oz) raw tiger prawns

75 g (3 oz) canned water chestnuts, drained and chopped

2.5 cm (1 inch) piece of fresh root ginger, peeled and grated

6 spring onions, finely chopped

1 teaspoon harissa

grated rind of 1 lime

125 g (4 oz) polenta or cornmeal

a little light olive oil, for frying

salt and pepper

Harissa dressing:

3 teaspoon harissa

3 tablespoons olive oil

juice of 1 lime

To serve:

4 mini pitta breads, sliced

1 lime, sliced

Serves 4
Preparation time: 20 minutes
Cooking time: 10 minutes

Skin and bone the fish then place it in a food processor with the prawns, water chestnuts, ginger, spring onions, harissa paste, grated lime rind and a little salt and pepper. Blitz until the mixture comes together but still has a rough texture. Divide the mixture into 8 portions and form into round burgers. Cover and chill for 1 hour.

Spread the polenta on a large plate. Dip the burgers into the polenta and coat evenly. Heat the oil in a shallow pan and fry the burgers for 8 minutes, turning frequently, until cooked through. Meanwhile, whisk together the dressing ingredients and set aside.

To assemble, wrap the pitta bread slices around the burgers, top each with a slice of lime and secure with a cocktail stick. Serve accompanied by the harissa dressing.

vegetarian

falafel burgers with hummus

425 g (14 oz) can chickpeas, drained and
   rinsed

2 garlic cloves, crushed

1 small red onion, finely chopped

2 teaspoons ground cumin

2 tablespoons chopped coriander

2 tablespoons chopped flat leaf parsley

grated rind of 1 lemon

1 egg yolk

2 tablespoons gram or plain flour

a little vegetable oil, for frying

salt and pepper

Garlic mint sauce:

200 ml (7 fl oz) natural yogurt

2 tablespoons chopped mint

1 garlic clove, crushed

To serve:

8 mini pitta breads

6 tablespoons red pepper hummus

1 bunch of watercress

2 tomatoes, cut into segments

¼ cucumber, sliced

Serves 4
Preparation time: 15 minutes, plus chilling
Cooking time: 8 minutes

Gram flour or besan is used in Indian cooking. It's made of ground, dried chickpeas, which gives it its pale yellow colour and high protein content. It's worth getting hold of and keeps well, refrigerated, for up to 6 months. You can buy red pepper hummus at the deli counters of most large supermarkets.

Place all the ingredients for the falafel, except the flour, in a food processor, season with salt and pepper and blitz until ground to a textured paste. Using slightly wet hands, divide the mixture into 8 balls then flatten them slightly to make burgers. Cover and chill for 30 minutes.

To make the garlic mint sauce, mix the yogurt with the mint and garlic. Season with salt and pepper and set aside until needed.

Lightly coat the burgers with the flour and shallow fry in the oil for 4 minutes on each side until golden brown and crisp.

To assemble, toast the pittas under a hot grill, spread each one with some hummus and top with salad and a burger. Serve with the garlic mint sauce.

spicy bean burgers

2 tablespoons light olive oil

1 small red onion, finely chopped

2 garlic cloves, crushed

1 yellow pepper, cored, deseeded and
  finely chopped

2 red chillies, deseeded and finely chopped

2 teaspoons paprika

1 teaspoon cayenne pepper

25 g (1 oz) wild rocket, finely chopped

2 tablespoons chopped parsley

1 tablespoon chopped thyme

1 small egg, beaten

1 tablespoon Tabasco sauce

50 g (2 oz) fresh breadcrumbs

2 x 425 g (14 oz) cans butter beans,
  drained and rinsed

a little vegetable oil, for frying

salt and pepper

To serve:

4 Soft Focaccia Rolls (*see page 85*)

salad leaves

1 quantity Tomato and Sweet Chilli Relish
  (*see page 94*)

Serves 4
Preparation time: 25 minutes, plus chilling
Cooking time: 10 minutes

Heat the oil in a medium pan and add the onion, garlic, pepper and chillies. Cover and simmer over a low-medium heat for 5 minutes or until the onion is cooked through but not coloured. Add the paprika, cayenne pepper, rocket, parsley and thyme and cook for 1 further minute. Remove from the heat and leave to cool.

Mix the onion mixture with the remaining burger ingredients and season well with salt and pepper. Mash with a potato masher until well combined. Divide the mixture into 4 portions and form into balls then flatten slightly into burgers. Cover and chill for 30 minutes.

Heat some vegetable oil in a shallow nonstick pan and fry the burgers for 3 minutes on each side or until heated through and slightly crisp. Drain well on kitchen paper.

To assemble, halve the rolls and toast under a grill then top each base with salad leaves and a burger. Serve with the lid and tomato and sweet chilli relish on the side.

sweet potato, butter bean and feta burger
with sun-blushed tomato pesto

500 g (1 lb) sweet potatoes, cut into 2 cm
(¾ inch) dice

300 g (10 oz) can butter beans, drained and
rinsed

150 g (5 oz) feta cheese

2 tablespoons chopped sage

1 tablespoon plain flour

1 egg, beaten

75 g (3 oz) panko or dried breadcrumbs

vegetable oil, for frying

salt and pepper

Sun-blushed tomato pesto

125 g (4 oz) sun-blushed tomatoes

15 g (½ oz) roasted pine nuts

3 tablespoons chopped basil leaves

3 tablespoons extra virgin olive oil

To serve:

4 burger buns or baps

salad leaves

toasted pine nuts

Serves 4
Preparation time: 25 minutes, plus chilling
Cooking time: 35 minutes

First, make the pesto by blending together all the pesto ingredients in a food processor until you have a textured paste.

Boil the sweet potatoes in salted boiling water for 15 minutes or until soft. Drain and leave to cool then mash the sweet potatoes with the butter beans using a potato masher. Fold in the feta and sage and season to taste with salt and pepper, remembering that the feta is quite salty. Divide into 4 portions and form into balls, then flatten slightly into burgers.

Coat the burgers in the flour, then dip them first in the beaten egg and then in the breadcrumbs. Re-form into a burger shape if necessary and then cover and chill for 30 minutes.

Heat the oil in a shallow pan and fry the burgers for 2–3 minutes or until golden brown crisp. Drain on kitchen paper.

To assemble, halve the buns or baps and toast under a grill. Top each base with some salad then a burger. Spoon over the pesto and pine nuts and serve immediately with extra pesto and the lid on the side.

crispy tofu burger

400 g (13 oz) firm tofu

3 tablespoons soy sauce

1 tablespoon rice wine vinegar

1 teaspoon sesame oil

2.5 cm (1 inch) piece of fresh root
   ginger, peeled and grated

1 garlic clove, crushed

2 large eggs, beaten

75 g (3 oz) fresh breadcrumbs

25 g (1 oz) sesame seeds

a little light olive oil, for frying

Roasted cherry tomatoes:

250 g (8 oz) cherry tomatoes

2 garlic cloves, chopped

2 tablespoons chopped basil

2 tablespoons olive oil

To serve:

4 crusty rolls

salad leaves

Serves 4

Preparation time: 20 minutes, plus
   marinating

Cooking time: 25 minutes

Cut the tofu into 4 square pieces and lay them flat in a non-metallic dish. Mix together the soy sauce, vinegar, sesame oil, ginger and garlic and pour over the tofu. Cover and leave to marinate for at least 1 hour, but preferably over night.

To cook the roasted cherry tomatoes, place the tomatoes into a roasting tin and scatter with the garlic, basil and olive oil. Cook in a preheated oven, 200°C (400°F) Gas Mark 6, until the skins start to split, about 15 minutes. Set aside until needed (the tomatoes can be eaten hot or at room temperature).

To make the burgers, dip the tofu into the beaten egg, then into the breadcrumbs and finally into the mixed sesame seeds. Dip each burger in the egg, then the breadcrumbs again for an extra thick coating.

Heat the oil in a shallow pan and fry the tofu burgers on each side over a medium-high heat until golden and crispy, about 6–8 minutes. Drain on kitchen paper.

To assemble, halve the rolls and toast under a grill. Top each base with salad leaves and a crispy tofu burger. Spoon over the roasted cherry tomatoes and their juices and serve immediately with the lids on the side.

portobello mushroom burger with goat's cheese

4 portobello mushrooms

2 garlic cloves, finely chopped

2 tablespoons chopped thyme

3 tablespoons olive oil

4 large slices of roasted red pepper

150 g (5 oz) goat's cheese, cut into
  4 thick slices

25–50 g (1–2 oz) butter

125 g (4 oz) fresh breadcrumbs

grated rind of 1 lemon

4 tablespoons finely chopped parsley

salt and pepper

To serve:

2 large burger buns

75 g (3 oz) rocket leaves, plus extra
  for garnish

Serves 4
Preparation time: 5 minutes
Cooking time: 20 minutes

Portobello mushrooms are large, flat mushrooms. They have a dense, meaty texture and rustic flavour that is perfect for this burger.

Place the mushrooms in a baking tin and sprinkle them with the garlic and thyme. Drizzle over the olive oil and cook in a preheated oven, 200°C (400°F) Gas Mark 6, for 10 minutes.

Place a slice of red pepper and a slice of goat's cheese on each mushroom. Heat the butter in a nonstick frying pan and fry the breadcrumbs, lemon rind and parsley until the breadcrumbs just start to colour, about 3 minutes. Spoon the breadcrumb mixture over the mushrooms and season well with salt and pepper. Return the burgers to the oven and roast for a further 5 minutes until the top is golden and the cheese has started to melt.

To assemble, halve the buns and toast under a grill. Top each half with rocket leaves and a mushroom. Garnish with extra rocket leaves and serve.

accompaniments

cajun sweet potato chips

2 sweet potatoes, finely sliced

4 tablespoons cornflour

2 tablespoons Cajun seasoning

a little vegetable oil, for deep frying

Serves 4
Preparation time: 10 minutes
Cooking time: 8–10 minutes

Place the sweet potato slices in a large bowl and add the cornflour and Cajun seasoning. Toss together well to lightly coat the chips.

Quarter-fill a large pan with vegetable oil and heat it to 180°C (350°F) or until a piece of bread browns in 30 seconds. Fry the potatoes in batches for 2 minutes until golden and crisp. Drain on lots of kitchen paper.

garlic and rosemary-flavoured fat chips

750 g (1½ lb) red potatoes

6 garlic cloves, skins on

3 tablespoons olive oil

2 tablespoons chopped rosemary

rock salt and pepper

Serves 4

Preparation time: 10 minutes

Cooking time: 40 minutes

Cut the potatoes into thick chips and put them in a large nonstick roasting tin. Crush the garlic cloves in their skins and scatter over the chips. Drizzle with the olive oil and season with rosemary, rock salt and pepper. Cook in a preheated oven, 200°C (400°F) Gas Mark 6, for 40 minutes, giving the chips a good shake every 10 minutes to prevent them from sticking.

When the chips are crisp and golden remove them from the oven, drain on kitchen paper and serve immediately.

straw parsnip chips with thyme

2 large parsnips
1 teaspoon dried thyme
1 tablespoon plain flour
vegetable oil, for deep-frying

Serves 4
Preparation time: 10 minutes
Cooking time: 8–10 minutes

Slice the parsnips very thinly, preferably using a mandolin with a thin julienne blade. Put the parsnip chips in a bowl and toss with the dried thyme and flour.

Quarter fill a large pan with vegetable oil and heat to 180°C (350°F) or until a piece of bread browns in 30 seconds. Fry the parsnips in batches for 2 minutes or until golden and crisp. Drain on lots of kitchen paper.

southern fried onion rings

3 onions, cut into 1 cm (¼ inch) rings

500 ml (17 fl oz) buttermilk

125 g (4 oz) plain flour

2 teaspoons sweet or ordinary paprika

1 teaspoon cayenne pepper

1 teaspoon freshly ground pepper

1 teaspoon rock salt

vegetable oil, for deep frying

Serves 4

Preparation time: 5 minutes, plus
  marinating

Cooking time: 8–10 minutes

When buying the buttermilk, go for one that is the consistency of pouring double cream. If you can't find sweet paprika, ordinary paprika will do fine for this recipe.

Place the onion rings in a large bowl and pour over the buttermilk. Leave to marinate for at least 30 minutes.

Mix together the flour, paprika, cayenne pepper, ground pepper and salt on a large plate.

Quarter-fill a large pan with vegetable oil and heat to 180°C (350°F) or until a piece of bread browns in 30 seconds.

Remove a small handful of onion rings from the buttermilk and coat in the seasoned flour. Cook the rings in the oil for 2 minutes or until golden brown. Drain well on kitchen paper and serve warm.

crusty sesame seed rolls

750 g (1½ lb) strong white flour, plus extra
  for dusting

7 g (¼ oz) sachet dried yeast

1 teaspoon salt

a pinch of sugar

450 ml (¾ pint) lukewarm water

Topping:

1 egg, beaten

½ tablespoon sesame seeds

½ tablespoon black sesame seeds

(or you could use sunflower seeds, chilli
  flakes, caraway seeds or poppy seeds)

Makes 10
Preparation time: 22 minutes, plus proving
Cooking time: 25 minutes

Creating a little steam in the oven while cooking the bread rolls will give the finished roll a crisper finish. A water spray is an ideal tool for this but pouring a little water on the bottom of the oven works just as well.

Sieve the flour into a large bowl and add the yeast, salt and sugar. Make a well in the centre and add most of the water, keeping back about 50 ml (2 fl oz). Mix thoroughly, adding the remaining water if necessary, until you have a firm, soft dough.

Knead the dough on a lightly floured surface for about 10 minutes, stretching and folding until it is smooth and elastic. Put the dough back in the bowl and cover with a clean, damp cloth. Put it in a warm place and leave to rise until doubled in size, about 50 minutes.

Turn out the dough and knock it back by kneading it for another 1–2 minutes. Divide the dough into 10 pieces and roll into round balls. Place the rolls on lightly floured trays allowing enough space for them to double in size. Lightly brush each roll with beaten egg and sprinkle half the rolls with the white sesame seeds and the other half with the black sesame seeds (or sprinkle with whatever seeds you are using). Cover and leave to prove until doubled in size, about 50 minutes.

Put the trays of bread in a preheated oven, 200°C (400°F) Gas Mark 6. Sprinkle about 125 ml, 4 fl oz water over the bottom of the oven to create a little steam. Close the door immediately and cook the rolls for 25 minutes or until golden and cooked through. If they are browning too fast, cover them lightly with foil. When the rolls are cooked, remove them from the oven and cool on a wire rack.

soft rolls

750 g (1½ lb) strong white flour, plus extra
  for dusting

1 teaspoon salt

a pinch of sugar

50 g (2 oz) butter

7 g (¼ oz) sachet of dried yeast

1 egg, beaten

450 ml (¾ pint) milk

Makes 10

Preparation time: 27 minutes, plus proving

Cooking time: 25 minutes

This recipe can easily be adapted to make a focaccia-style bread by adding olive oil and and flattening the dough before baking *(see below)*.

Sieve the flour, salt and sugar into a large bowl. Rub the butter into the flour until it resembles fine breadcrumbs. Stir in the dried yeast, egg and enough milk to form a soft, slightly sticky dough. Knead the dough on a floured surface for 10 minutes, stretching and folding until it is smooth and elastic. Put the dough back in the bowl and cover with a clean, damp cloth. Leave to rise in a warm place until doubled in size, about 50 minutes.

Knock back the dough by kneading it for another 1–2 minutes. Divide the dough into 10 equal pieces then roll them into round balls. Place the rolls on lightly floured trays, allowing enough space for them to double in size.

Lightly dust each roll with a little flour and bake in a preheated oven, 200°C (400°F) Gas Mark 6, for 25 minutes or until golden and cooked through. Leave to cool slightly on a wire rack before serving.

Soft focaccia rolls

Make the bread as above but using 25 ml (1 fl oz) olive oil instead of the butter.

When you have shaped the dough into rolls, flatten them slightly and press your fingers into the dough to make 8 dents in the surface.

Drizzle with more oil and sprinkle with rock salt and chopped rosemary. Leave to prove as for the rolls and bake in the same way.

asian salad

1 bunch of spring onions, shredded

50 g (2 oz) bean sprouts

3 Baby Gem lettuces, leaves separated

1 cucumber, cut into ribbons with a
    vegetable peeler

1 small bunch of mint, torn

1 small bunch of basil, torn

1 small bunch of coriander, torn

Dressing:

2 tablespoons light olive oil

grated rind and juice of 1 lime

1 large red chilli, deseeded and finely
    chopped

1 tablespoon Asian fish sauce

1 tablespoon light soy sauce

a pinch of sugar

Serves 4
Preparation time: 10 minutes, plus cooling

The fish sauce in this dressing gives the salad an authentic Asian flavour. You can use nam pla, nuoc mam or nuoc nam and can find it in most supermarkets or Asian stores.

Place the shredded spring onions and bean sprouts in iced water and leave for 30 minutes, then remove and drain well.

In a large serving bowl, toss the onion and sprouts with the lettuce leaves, cucumber and herbs.

Whisk together the ingredients for the dressing in a small bowl and pour over the salad. Serve immediately.

fennel and orange salad

1 large head chicory

1 large head radicchio

3 oranges, segmented

2 small fennel bulbs

½ pomegranate

Dressing:

3 tablespoons olive oil

1 tablespoon aged red wine vinegar

1 tablespoon clear honey

salt and pepper

Serves 4

Preparation time: 15 minutes

Using an aged vinegar will give much more depth of flavour without adding overpowering acidity. It's a product that's well worth having in your storecupboard.

To make the dressing, whisk together the olive oil, vinegar and honey. Season with salt and pepper and set aside until needed.

Separate the chicory and radicchio into leaves and arrange on a large platter. Finely slice the fennel and layer with the orange slices over the salad leaves.

Drizzle over the dressing, scatter with the pomegranate seeds and serve.

red cabbage coleslaw with almonds and wholegrain mustard dressing

¼ red cabbage

1 small red onion, finely sliced

1 carrot, grated

1 orange pepper, cored, deseeded and
  shredded

50 g (2 oz) sliced almonds, dry roasted

salt and pepper

Wholegrain mustard dressing:

juice of 1 orange

1 tablespoon wholegrain mustard

1 garlic clove, crushed

3 tablespoons olive oil

Serves 4

Preparation time: 20 minutes

Remove the core and outer leaves from the cabbage and finely shred with a sharp knife or push through the shredder attachment on a food processor. In a large bowl, mix the cabbage with the onion, carrot, orange pepper and almonds.

Whisk together all the ingredients for the dressing and toss with the shredded vegetables. Season well with salt and pepper and leave to stand for 30 minutes before serving.

baby spinach, pear and garlic crispbread salad
with a blue cheese dressing

1 small French baguette

2 garlic cloves, crushed

2 tablespoons olive oil

125 g (4 oz) baby spinach leaves

1 ripe pear, cut into fine wedges

Blue cheese dressing:

1 tablespoon lemon juice

50 g (2 oz) soft blue cheese, such as
  Roquefort

1 tablespoon mayonnaise

3 tablespoons crème fraîche or
  soured cream

Serves 4
Preparation time: 15 minutes
Cooking time: 10 minutes

Slice the baguette at an angle into slices that are so thin you can just see through the bread.

Mix together the garlic and oil and brush over the bread. Place the bread on a baking sheet and bake in a preheated oven, 200°C (400°F) Gas Mark 6, for 10 minutes or until crisp and golden. Leave to cool.

To serve, arrange the spinach, pear and crisp garlic toast on a large serving platter. Whisk together all the ingredients for the dressing and drizzle over the salad.

rocket, beetroot and red pepper salad
with a roasted hazelnut and balsamic dressing

4 medium raw beetroots

1 tablespoon olive oil

75 g (3 oz) rocket leaves

300 g (10 oz) jar chargrilled red peppers,
  drained

Roasted hazelnut and balsamic
  dressing:

50 g (2 oz) roasted hazelnuts, roughly
  chopped

1 tablespoon balsamic vinegar

1 garlic clove, crushed

4 tablespoons light olive oil or hazelnut oil

salt and pepper

Serves 4
Preparation time: 10 minutes
Cooking time: 1¼ hours

Cook the beetroots in salted boiling water for 45 minutes or until just cooked, then drain. Peel off the skin under cold running water. Cut each beetroot into 6–8 segments and arrange in a roasting dish. Drizzle with the oil and roast in a preheated oven, 200°C (400°F) Gas Mark 6 for 30 minutes or until cooked through and slightly charred around the edges.

To make the dressing, blitz half the hazelnuts with the vinegar, garlic and oil in a food processor until smooth. Season well with salt and pepper.

Place the rocket leaves, red pepper and roasted beetroot on a large plate and scatter over the remaining hazelnuts. Drizzle the dressing over the salad and serve immediately.

quick bbq sauce

250 ml (8 fl oz) tomato ketchup

125 ml (4 fl oz) tomato purée

125 ml (4 fl oz) apple cider vinegar

4 tablespoons blackstrap molasses

1 tablespoon Worcestershire sauce

1 teaspoon Dijon mustard

1 teaspoon Tabasco sauce (or Chipotle
  Tabasco)

Makes 450 ml (¾ pint)
Preparation time: 5 minutes
Cooking time: 10 minutes

This classic sauce will go with most burgers. Chipotle Tabasco sauce, if you can find it, has a smoky yet subtle chilli flavour which works well in this recipe.

Place all ingredients in a saucepan and simmer over a medium heat for 5–10 minutes or until thick. Pour into sterilized jars and leave to cool. Use immediately or store in the refrigerator for up to 2 weeks.

tomato ketchup

3 kg (6 lb) ripe tomatoes, roughly chopped

1 onion, chopped

1 garlic clove, chopped

1 red pepper, deseeded and chopped

250 ml (8 fl oz) cider vinegar

200 g (7 oz) sugar

1 tablespoon green peppercorns

1 teaspoon salt

1 teaspoon English mustard powder

½ teaspoon ground allspice

½ teaspoon cayenne pepper

¼ teaspoon ground cloves or
  5 whole cloves

Makes 600 ml (1 pint)
Preparation time: 20 minutes
Cooking time: 2½ hours

Making your own ketchup takes a little time but the lack of artificial sweeteners and preservatives makes a far superior sauce and is well worth the effort.

Place all the ingredients into a heavy-based saucepan and bring to the boil. Simmer over a medium heat for 35 minutes, stirring frequently.

Remove the pan from the heat, cover and leave to rest for 1–2 hours. This will allow the flavours to blend together.

Push the mixture through a fine sieve, discarding the mushy skins left in the sieve. Wash out the pan and pour in the sieved tomato mixture. Bring back to the boil and simmer the ketchup over a low heat until thick, about 1½ hours, stirring occasionally.

Pour the ketchup into dry sterilized bottles or jars, seal and cool. Use immediately or store for up to 1 month in the refrigerator.

mayonnaise

2 large egg yolks
1 teaspoon English mustard powder
a good pinch of salt
1–2 tablespoons lemon juice
175 ml (6 fl oz) groundnut oil
100 ml (3½ fl oz) olive oil

Makes 300 ml (½ pint)
Preparation time: 20 minutes

Whisk together the yolks, mustard, salt and lemon juice in a bowl, preferably one with a narrow base. Place the bowl on a damp cloth, to help hold it steady, so you have a free hand to pour in the oil. Alternatively, use a blender or liquidizer.

When the yolks have blended start adding the oils a few drop at a time, whisking well between each addition. Once the mixture starts to thicken, you can start pouring in the oil a very thin, steady stream. If the mayonnaise curdles, simply whisk another yolk in a clean bowl and slowly add the curdled sauce to it, whisking continuously. If you are using a blender, gradually add the oil while blending at the same time.

When you have added all the oil, check the taste and consistency, adding lemon juice for sharpness and salt and mustard to taste. For a lighter consistency, whisk in 1–2 tablespoons of boiling water.

Additional Flavours

Garlic or Aïoli Add 5 crushed garlic cloves to the yolk mixture before you start adding the oil.

Dijon or Wholegrain Mustard Add 1 tablespoon of either Dijon or wholegrain mustard to the yolk mixture before you start adding the oil. Stir through more mustard at the end, to taste.

Mixed Herbs Stir 4 tablespoons freshly chopped mixed herbs, such as parsley, chives and basil, into the finished mayonnaise.

Basil Stir 4 tablespoons freshly chopped basil into the finished mayonnaise.

Lemon Stir 2 tablespoons grated lemon rind through the mixture. Add a few drops of lemon juice to lighten the mixture.

Horseradish Stir 1 tablespoon creamed horseradish through the finished mayonnaise.

smoky pepper relish

2 red peppers, cored, halved and deseeded

1 yellow pepper, cored, halved and
   deseeded

2 tablespoons chopped basil

1½ tablespoons balsamic vinegar

3 tablespoon olive oil

3 garlic cloves, sliced

1 teaspoon smoked paprika

salt and pepper

Makes 350 ml (12 fl oz)
Preparation time: 20 minutes
Cooking time: 25 minutes

Grill the peppers under a preheated hot grill until the skins are black. Transfer to a heatproof bowl and cover tightly with clingfilm. Leave to cool then peel off and discard the skins.

Finely slice the peppers and put them into a bowl with the basil and balsamic vinegar.

Heat the oil and fry the garlic and paprika until the garlic is just starting to brown then pour the oil over the peppers. Season with salt and pepper and mix well.

Spoon the relish into a clean jar and use immediately or it can be stored in the refrigerator for up to a week.

tomato and sweet chilli relish

5 large red chillies, deseeded and chopped

3 garlic cloves, chopped

500 g (1 lb) tomatoes, diced

125 g (4 oz) sugar

125 ml (4 fl oz) red wine vinegar

Makes 300 ml (½ pint)
Preparation time: 15 minutes
Cooking time: 45 minutes

Place the chillies, garlic and half the tomatoes in a food processor and blitz until puréed.

Pour the purée into a large heavy-based pan with the sugar, vinegar and remaining tomatoes. Bring to the boil and simmer for about 40–45 minutes or until thick, stirring occasionally. Set aside to cool slightly.

Pour the relish into clean jars and seal. This relish will keep in the refrigerator for up to 2 weeks.

butter bean, tomato and coriander salsa

300 g (10 oz) can butter beans, drained
and rinsed

3 medium plum tomatoes, diced

1 large red chilli, deseeded and
finely chopped

1 large green chilli, deseeded and
finely chopped

2 garlic cloves, finely chopped

juice and grated rind of 1 lime

2 tablespoons olive oil

3 tablespoons chopped coriander

salt and pepper

Makes 450 ml (¾ pint)

**Preparation time: 15 minutes, plus
standing**

Mix the butter beans with all the remaining of the ingredients and season well with salt and pepper. Leave to infuse for 30 minutes then serve.

index

acknowledgements

Executive editor Sarah Ford
Editor Emma Pattison
Executive art editor and design Geoff Fennell
Photographer Stephen Conroy
Home economist Sunil Vijayakar
Stylist Rachel Jukes
Production controller Nigel Reed